P9-CND-477

SHAPING A PRESIDENT

SCULPTING
FOR THE
ROOSEVELT
MEMORIAL

KELLI PEDUZZI

PHOTOGRAPHS BY DIANE SMOOK

THE MILLBROOK PRESS
BROOKFIELD, CONNECTICUT

Allen County Public Library
900 Webster Street
PO Box 2270
Fort Wayne, IN

Published by The Millbrook Press
2 Old New Milford Road
Brookfield, Connecticut 06804

Text copyright © 1997 by Kelli Peduzzi
Photographs copyright © 1997 by Diane Smook
All rights reserved
Printed in the United States of America
6 5 4 3 2 1

Library of Congress Cataloging-in-Publication Data
Peduzzi, Kelli.
Shaping a president : sculpting for the Roosevelt Memorial / by
Kelli Peduzzi ; photographs by Diane Smook.
p.   cm.
Summary: Follows the work of the sculptor Neil Estern during the
creation of the memorial in Washington, D.C. which features the former
president, first lady, and their dog Fala.
ISBN 0-7613-0207-7 (lib. bdg.) 0-7613-0325-1 (pbk.)
1. Estern, Neil—Criticism and interpretation—Juvenile literature.
2. Roosevelt, Franklin D. (Franklin Delano) 1882-1945—Portraits—
Juvenile literature. 3. Roosevelt, Eleanor, 1884-1962—Portraits—
Juvenile literature. 4. Fala (Dog)—Juvenile literature.
5. Animal sculpture—Washington (D.C.)—Juvenile literature.
6. Franklin Delano Roosevelt Memorial (Washington, D.C.)
7. Washington (D.C.)—Buildings, structures, etc. [1. Estern, Neil.
2. Roosevelt, Franklin D. (Franklin Delano), 1882-1945.
3. Roosevelt, Eleanor, 1884-1962. 4. Fala (Dog) 5. Franklin Delano
Roosevelt Memorial (Washington, D.C.) 6. National monuments.]
I. Smook, Diane, ill.
NB237.E75P44 1997
730'.92—DC21   97-7331 CIP AC

Book design by Tania Garcia
Text is set in 12 pt. Goudy

For Bob, Edward, James, and Julian, the men in our lives.

We would like to acknowledge Neil and Anne Estern for their loyal assistance and cooperation, as well as Greg Glasson and the staff of Tallix Fine Arts Foundry for their continual support. We also wish to thank Amy Shields, our editor, for her unwavering enthusiasm and good judgment.

W hen I realized that I was actually going to get to sculpt for the Roosevelt Memorial," says artist Neil Estern, "I was a little intimidated. It's a big responsibility. It would be compared to other memorials in Washington. As an artist I thought, 'I could do that,' but also, 'Can I really do it?'"

Estern had been chosen by the memorial's architect, Lawrence Halprin, as one of five sculptors whose work would appear in the Franklin Delano Roosevelt Memorial in Washington, D.C. "Originally he wanted only one sculptor, but thought it would take too long for one person to do it all. So he chose the five of us: Leonard Baskin, Robert Graham, George Segal, Tom Hardy and me. Little did we know it would take almost twenty years to finish anyway."

Something grand was needed to honor the president who had led the nation through the Great Depression and World War II. Roosevelt had loved gardens, so the architect designed a park on the Potomac Tidal Basin, close to the Jefferson Memorial. The park would be outlined by red granite walls making up four outdoor "rooms," one for each of FDR's presidential terms. Waterfalls would play a central role, adding soothing sounds to the garden. "The design has a timeless quality," says Neil. "It could have been built as Solomon's temple or far in the future. In a memorial that's a great advantage. You don't want it to go out of style." But what sort of sculpture should it hold?

"We held a week of meetings at Halprin's San Francisco office," recounts Neil. "Who wanted to do what? My immediate reaction was, 'I want to do Roosevelt.' Segal wanted to do the common folk from life. So he sculpted the farm couple, the Depression breadline, and the fireside chat. Graham, well, he's known for doing the female nude. He didn't want to do a portrait." So he agreed to do the reliefs of the first inauguration, at which Roosevelt uttered his memorable encouragement, "The only thing we have to fear is fear itself." Baskin contributed a relief of the funeral procession, and Tom Hardy would sculpt the presidential seal. "So I realized, gee, that left me. I got stuck with the portraits of FDR, Eleanor, and Fala," says a smiling Neil. "I knew I could do it; still I was overawed at the magnitude of it." Money shortages and design delays slowed the project. It wasn't until Congress set aside the funds in 1985 that Neil could finally get down to the business of sculpting.

A sculptor needs plenty of space in which to work. This space, his studio, must be big enough to hold tables, tools, and supplies, as well as the enormous sculptures themselves. Neil's Brooklyn studio, the top floor of his brownstone, is fairly small: 18 feet (5.5 meters) long, 21 feet (6.5 meters) wide, and 21 feet high.

Since the sculptures he makes are two and three times life-size, Neil also uses ladders. "I can't move a big sculpture up and down," he says, "but I can move up and down." When he's ready to apply clay to the head and upper body of a large model, up the ladder he climbs.

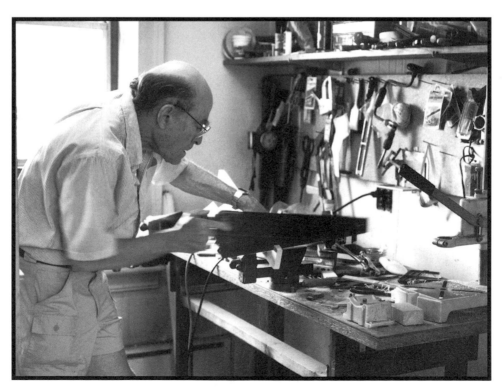

Neil starts work at 9 a.m., stopping at 12:30 to eat lunch and take a walk. After lunch, he works for another three to four hours. The radio plays classical music while he sculpts. "Sculpting is a series of small decisions," he explains. "Should it go this way or that way?"

Light is the next most important thing in an artist's studio. Neil's wall of skylights faces north. Northern light is the best for artists to create in, because it is steady; it casts few shadows and little glare. Beneath the skylights is a row of fluorescent lights with special bulbs that imitate daylight. Neil uses these on cloudy or rainy days. Good light is the key to sculpting a three-dimensional object—something with height, width, and depth. To see an entire painting, you need only to stand in front of it. But to see a sculpture properly, you have to be able to walk around it and see it from all sides.

The sculptor learns how to read a surface by the way light casts and creates the illusion of depth. When the object is correctly lighted, Neil can see exactly how much to make a surface curve. The ability to translate these light impressions into rounded clay forms is especially important in trying to sculpt someone's likeness.

A lucky sculptor will have a live subject to measure and touch. Body gestures, facial expressions, and posture are all part of the way people look. But Neil has only photographs to work with. Roosevelt's face varied from photo to photo. "I have real trouble with the nose," explains Neil. "The bone structure is difficult to work out. None of the existing bronze busts of him are the same, so I can't rely on those. The few posed photos of him are altered and look phony. I've compared dozens of photos to see which elements of his nose repeat themselves. It is hard detective work, slow and tiring."

The next hurdle is deciding Roosevelt's pose. Neil uses photographs of the president at the Yalta Summit Conference in January 1945. There Roosevelt appeared seated, wrapped in his navy cape, looking haggard from years of overwork. Neil pores over many photos of FDR, each one giving the sculptor a slightly different angle on the president's physique.

Hardest of all is how to show FDR's body, paralyzed from the waist down by polio. Polio removed the use of his legs, but he was never seen in public in a wheelchair. He was usually supported by a family member and wore leg

braces as he stood, or he appeared seated in a regular chair. So the sculptor chooses to seat the president in his favorite chair. The ornate chair with the Roosevelt family crest carved on the back is one of a dining-room set at Roosevelt's home in Hyde Park, New York. It was fitted out with small wheels. In this chair FDR wheeled himself short distances through the house, even going out to the large front porch to greet neighbors and well-wishers.

Neil wants to suggest the disability, but doesn't want it to be the first thing that people notice. Indeed, both in public and private life the president always acted like it wasn't there. "Roosevelt was a proud man," notes the sculptor, "and very concerned with presenting himself in the most positive light possible. He never wished to appear helpless and dependent on others. He was always upbeat and full of high spirits. He used his wit, charm, and sense of humor even more after the polio to distract you from the fact that he was incapacitated. His eldest grandson, Curtis, told me that when he lived in the White House as a teenager his grandfather refused to be pitied. Family members did not dare discuss infirmities of any kind. Especially during the war FDR was at great pains to give the impression of invincibility. This was obviously something he felt was important. While he did not

deny that he had polio, it was something he refused to emphasize in any way. As a sculptor trying to do an evocative portrait of the man, I would naturally choose to show him as he presented himself and how he was perceived by most Americans. To me it would be an insult to the man's memory to do exactly the opposite of how he would want to be seen."

Still, polio enters into the sculpting process as Neil tries to show Roosevelt's unique body language. "Capturing the personality through the body is the most challenging part of sculpting," says Neil. "FDR did not move from the waist down, so he would shift his upper body dramatically. He had developed his upper body strength. He had a tremendously expressive face, too." From studying films of FDR, Neil notices how the president tossed his head and used his voice to create effect. "I try to show him this way, turning, about to speak to someone." Sitting in a dining-room chair before a mirror, Neil poses to create the body position and sketches it. Then FDR's cape, borrowed from Hyde Park, is draped around a cooperative friend until it falls just the way Neil wants to sculpt it. It's the most complex pose Neil has yet done.

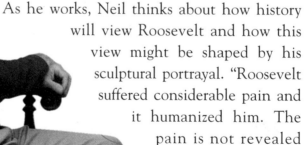

As he works, Neil thinks about how history will view Roosevelt and how this view might be shaped by his sculptural portrayal. "Roosevelt suffered considerable pain and it humanized him. The pain is not revealed but it's there. We were fortunate as a nation

3 1833 03224 5117

that despite his personal and physical flaws, he had the courage during the war to rise above this pain and lead the country." To portray FDR's character, the artist relies on instinct. "I think about the man as I work, and it all goes into the work, but I'm not sure just how sometimes. It's a very mysterious process. If you don't have any strong feelings about a person, even negative feelings, it's hard to sculpt them. I don't invent things about a person. I find things in their personality to bring out. FDR was a very charming man. This softened his calculating political side. The people responded to his twinkle. He was aristocratic, but his charisma made him accessible to the common man."

With the pose sketched, modeling begins. Neil creates three models before the statue is ready for casting. He starts small, and each successive model grows bigger and more detailed. First, Neil makes a 20-inch (50-centimeter) high study model, or maquette, based on his sketch. To do this, he builds a supporting structure called an armature by bending aluminum wire into the desired shape, carving wood and Styrofoam pieces, and fitting them all together. Upon this base, the details of the pose, facial expression, and clothing can take shape in plastiline clay.

Sculptors' clay has four grades of firmness from 1 (soft) to 4 (very firm). Soft clay, easy to spread, goes on wide areas. Firm clay is used where fine detail is needed. Neil kneads the clay to make it soft and workable and uses his strong thumbs to press small lumps of clay onto the armature, until it is covered. This is long, hard work. "My neck and thumbs hurt. With such a large sculpture, I feared physical strain, but I do exercises to help me strengthen the muscles."

As he shapes the clay, Neil says that his hands just seem to know instinctively what to do to create a true likeness, though he constantly has to exercise his judgment. "It's intensive work, and I must be very dedicated and self-critical to make sure it's right," says Neil. "But no art can be 100 percent conscious; it must also be intuitive. My hands and my brain are collaborating mysteriously. I never get tired of my subject. I get deeper and deeper into it the more I work on it." Once the clay covers the armature, Neil uses a wooden spatula, a metal scraper, and other small tools to shape the details. With the maquette finished, Neil makes a plaster cast of it and paints it green to look like a weathered bronze statue. He repeats this process for Eleanor and FDR's dog, Fala.

Neil then makes a model of the memorial site out of wood, cardboard, building paper, and glue to represent stone, brick, and mortar. He can move the maquettes around on this miniature stage set to help him get a feeling for how the statues will look in their final location. Neil places paper cut-outs made from pictures of his wife and children in front of the maquette to see how real people will look next to the size of the finished statue. After architect Halprin studies this diorama, Neil builds a second model to show a slightly smaller Roosevelt in the alcove. Still, the finished Roosevelt will be an imposing 8 feet 7.5 inches (263 centimeters) tall.

After looking at the maquette, Neil and Halprin make other refinements. These changes will show up in the scale model. Using the same materials and techniques, only in much greater quantity and detail, Neil painstakingly perfects the scale model, which at 35 inches (89 centimeters) tall is about one-third the size of the finished sculpture. Seventy pounds of plastiline and untold hours go into the scale model. The chair alone takes three months of exacting measurement, delicate carpentry, and precise rendering. Such

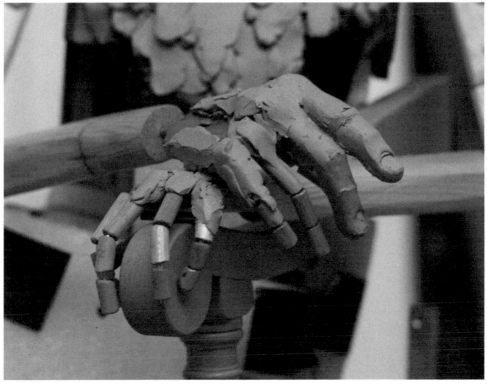

careful detailing at this stage prevents having to make drastic and costly changes at stage three, the enlargement, the final phase before moldmaking. Even slight changes result in major sculpting tasks. During the creation of the scale model, the commission votes to incline FDR's platform by an inch to allow water runoff. Because of this Neil has to saw off the chair legs and adjust the sculpture's entire perspective to allow for the tilt.

Neil constructs the scale model in five separate pieces: the chair, head, torso, cape with its toggle fastener, and legs. These are screwed together so that Neil can remove parts of the sculpture to put fine detail on hard-to-reach areas such as the deep spaces under the cape. This detail is needed because on the large final form, Neil does not want huge rough areas. He is thinking ahead to the casting process as well. The five pieces will be cast separately. If the figure were poured all in one piece, it would be far too heavy to manage, and uneven cooling would form holes in the sculpture.

Neil finishes FDR and turns his attention to the two other figures. Eleanor Roosevelt is the first first lady ever to be represented in a national monument. This is due to her great influence on FDR's presidency, especially the social reforms of the New Deal. As a tribute to her

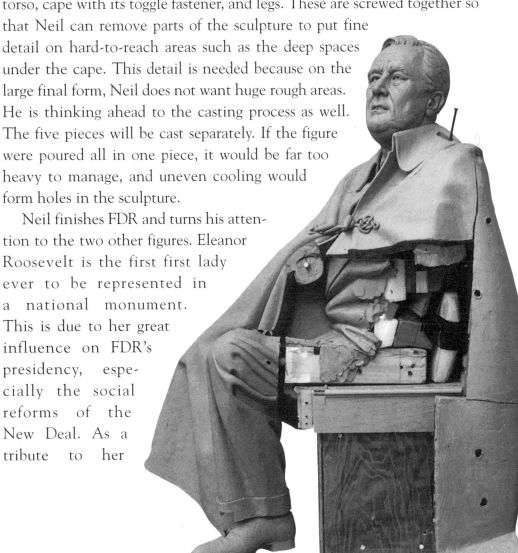

work, Halprin has given her a niche of her own near the president. Hers is a much straighter, simpler pose than her husband's voluminous triangular shape, and easier to sculpt. The scale model shows a middle-aged Eleanor wearing her favorite tweed coat. Her body is pulled up tall, poised as if to speak. "I do feel that she's looking at me," Neil says of the model's uncanny ability to follow a person's gaze about the room, "and that's what I'm after. I want the viewer to feel her vitality without the sense that she is a carbon copy of the person."

Roosevelt's beloved pet, Fala, is next to get Neil's attention. The sculptor had not meant to do the president's dog at first. Dogs have appeared in paintings for centuries, but rarely in memorial sculptures. Horses were the animals chosen to impart drama to statues of kings and nobles. But Senator Carl Levin urged him to do it. "I'm not an animal sculptor," admits the artist, "but when I found out that Levin was on the committee that would appropriate the money for the memorial, I thought, 'Maybe I can learn to sculpt dogs.'" Neil hopes to capture Fala's noble side, as befitting the dog of a great president. "I'm trying not to make him too cute," says Neil. "His tongue isn't sticking out. He's alert and regal, the same as FDR. Still, he is kind of cute. He's a Scotty, after all."

Fala presents Neil with a whole new set of challenges, despite the sculpture's fairly small size. The finished bronze of Fala will be 28 inches (71 centimeters) high, twice the size of the real dog. Neil observes a neighbor's Scotty to understand its bone and muscle structure. This part is fairly simple for an experienced artist. But the fur! Neil consults photos of Fala and even Renaissance sculpture to learn more about sculpting fur. It turns out to be very tricky to make a furry-looking dog in clay and bronze.

Adding to Neil's problem is that Fala, like most Scotties of his time, was not as well-groomed as his breed is now. "I look at Scotties today, but they don't look like Fala," says Neil. "They are shaved. Fala was hardly ever groomed. They trimmed him once a year." Not being brushed often, the artist says, made the dog's fur stick out. But Neil does not want to make Fala's hair spiky enough to poke a child who sits on his back. "I'm just trying to make it flow, and still look like a Scotty dog of the period."

With the scale models finished to his precise standards, Neil's hardest work is done. He and his wife, Anne, throw a good-bye party for them in

his studio. The figures are ready to be taken to the Tallix Foundry in Beacon, New York, for enlargement, coincidentally only minutes away from FDR's home in Hyde Park.

The foundry building is the size of a city block. The place hums with artists and foundry technicians at work. The sounds of banging tools, grinding motors, and the whoosh of torches and polishers fill the giant shed. The smells of scorched wax, oily clay, and damp plaster attack the nose. Everywhere one looks, light and color hit the eye. Sculptures both gigantic and tiny, shiny and dull, colorful and drab, realistic and abstract, fill all available floor space. Every surface is covered with clay and plaster dust, blobs of paint, wax, and metal. It's a beautiful mess.

In the enlarging room, a Tallix artisan named Harry Bachman creates another armature, huge but made of steel and lightweight Styrofoam. This way, less clay can be used, so the model is less likely to bend. Even so, more than 400 pounds (180 kilograms) of clay covers the final model, spread much thinner and over a much larger surface area than on previous models.

Next, an amazing process called pointing takes place. The pointing machine is an enlarging tool with two arms: the small arm set on the scale model, the large arm on the enlargement. The artisan moves the small arm

over the scale model, marking points along the surface at regular intervals. At the same time, the large arm is moving over the corresponding surface of the enlargement, marking the same points. The large arm actually carves into the clay so that a near-replica of the scale model is created without having to start from scratch, saving months of work. The deep interior spaces of the figure are also pointed by unscrewing and taking apart the five sections of the model as needed. Enlarging takes three months, but it is still not an exact replica. Neil works at the foundry for another eight months to hand-finish the surfaces of FDR in minute detail. He pays close attention to every fingernail, wrinkle, and wart. Hair must look "hairy." Muscles in the face have to be brought out. The pinky ring has to be right.

Neil makes more drastic changes than he expected at this stage. The translation from the scale model to the giant figure made some parts look out of whack. The hands are twice as big as intended, for instance. "Whenever you make something in a smaller size and it's enlarged three times, there are things that you become aware of that you weren't as sensitive to in the smaller model. Before you know it, you're moving a lot of clay around."

Neil compares close-up shots of FDR's hands with the enlargement, running his fingers over the sculpture to feel the angle of the clay. He pulls off hunks of clay with tools. This takes a lot of muscle as the clay is very firm. Neil removes 2 inches (50 millimeters) from the kneecap of the left leg to

make it more obvious that it's a withered limb. "I have to show that there's not much meat in there," he says. Photographs of both the president and first lady show that they had bad teeth and primitive dental work. Neil becomes something of a clay-wielding orthodontist.

Neil can't get close enough to the head by standing on a ladder. Yet fine detailing is called for. So FDR's head has been embedded with a steel loop. A giant hook on a pulley suspended from the foundry ceiling lifts the head off the body and sets it down where Neil can work easily. Neil further decides that the central composition formed by the triangle of the cape, head, and legs must look more imposing. FDR's right leg must be raised, the head and collar moved an inch to the left. The shoes need a lot of polishing. More clay is applied to the bottom edge of the cape to extend the triangle by 6 inches (150 millimeters). All of these sculpting decisions are made amid the noise, the lights, and people coming and going.

Neil is under pressure to finish, but these details continue to grip him. "I don't feature taking shortcuts," he declares. "It's taken me twice as long as I figured to perfect the FDR enlargement. Every time I think I'm making progress, I look at it and think, 'Oh, I still have work to do on the back of the cape' or, 'The shoes!' or 'The hair needs more work.'" Still, he is grateful to be able to sit down at the end of each twelve-hour day spent standing, pushing clay around, and climbing ladders. In his leisure moments he admits to a fanciful wish to sculpt his self-portrait into a fold of the cape, as Renaissance sculptors did. "I don't see where it could go, though I will have to sign it somewhere. Can't you just see a big 'E' in the middle of FDR's pinky ring?" he jokes.

Foundry work is further slowed by the confusion all around him. Neil can't see the outline of FDR with the visual chaos created by equipment and other sculptures in the background. He designs and has the Tallix staff build a two-story-high black screen. This gets rid of some background distractions and gives him a corner of privacy in the giant shed.

One unexpected sculpting tool that Neil discovers at the foundry is the bust of FDR made in 1933 by Joe Davidson, a leading portrait sculptor of the day. It is a young FDR, but as Neil has few three-dimensional records of his subject to rely on, he uses the bust to help him shape FDR's head. Neil measures the face to the last millimeter. Davidson's likeness of FDR is striking, but, says Neil, "It's a portrait without an inside. The psychological realism is not there. That just wasn't a concern of sculptors then like it is now."

As the enlargement nears completion in the spring of 1996, the memorial commission is beset on all sides by people arguing over how much to show FDR's polio. Neil continues his work, uncertain and anxious that after ten years of hard work on FDR, he might have to start over: "We are paying tribute to the man and his accomplishments and his role in American history," Neil observes. "His private afflictions are not part of the public persona and not part of the way people remember him. I'm doing what I consider visual biography, and I wouldn't change the facts of FDR's public life. I am sympathetic to the concerns of disabled people, but this should not affect how we regard history."

The commission decides to make a reproduction of the wheelchair that FDR used at Hyde Park, a wooden kitchen chair with bicycle tires. This will be placed in the entry building of the memorial.

With the FDR enlargement perfected, it is sent to the molding department, while Neil turns to finishing the enlargements of Eleanor and Fala.

Everyone at the foundry breathes a sigh of relief. They've been waiting for months to get their hands on the sculpture. The pace gets faster now that the messy process of making the first, or mother, mold begins.

Two casting methods are to be used on the gigantic figure. The largest and heaviest of the sections, the cape and the chair, will be sandcast. Sand-casting, says Kurt Rutter, a moldmaker at Tallix, is the way most machine parts are made for large factories. The process is relatively fast and inexpensive. Neil saves time and money at this stage by having divided the huge figure into five pieces.

The cape and chair are moved into another part of the foundry to begin the molding. The pieces are coated with several thin layers of liquid plastic called black tuffy. The rubbery tuffy will reproduce the sensitive details of the clay. Foundry workers Mike Keropian, a sculptor himself, and Tina Jeter, who was trained as a dental technician, get to work. They wear white coveralls, even over their boots. Strips of burlap cloth are soaked in large vats of liquid plaster. Mike and Tina apply the plaster-soaked strips with loud, wet slaps. From time to time they also fasten bits of tubing called rebar onto the plaster coating. "The burlap is like muscles," explains Mike, "and the tubes

are the bones. We're kind of making a skeleton to hold the sculpture together." When they have made the plaster layer an inch thick, they let it dry.

The large sections are now laid into a sandpit, and sand is filled in around them. A metal frame is placed around the pieces. Then a chemical hardener is added to a liquid plastic, called urethane. The mixture is poured over the sand until the sand is completely soaked with it. The plastic-sand mix hardens quickly—in about four hours—into something as hard as sandstone, with the tuffy mold of the cape and chair embedded into it. These sections are heavy—from 6,000 to 8,000 pounds (2,700 to 3,600 kilograms). A machine hoists them to the casting area. All traces of the clay are cleaned out of the tuffy mold and the pieces are put back together. The bronze can be poured straight into this mold. Nothing more needs to be prepared.

The other sections of FDR—the head, legs, hands, and feet have a lot of fine detail. These will be molded using the lost-wax process. Several thick coatings of black tuffy are brushed on carefully. The mold of FDR's left shoe is so black and shiny that it looks like real patent leather. Plaster and tubing jackets are also made for these sections to hold them firmly in place.

Though FDR's head will also be cast in lost-wax, it is given a more special treatment. While Mike and Tina are busy in the plaster room, Kurt Rutter first applies tuffy and then a "clay blanket" over FDR's head. The

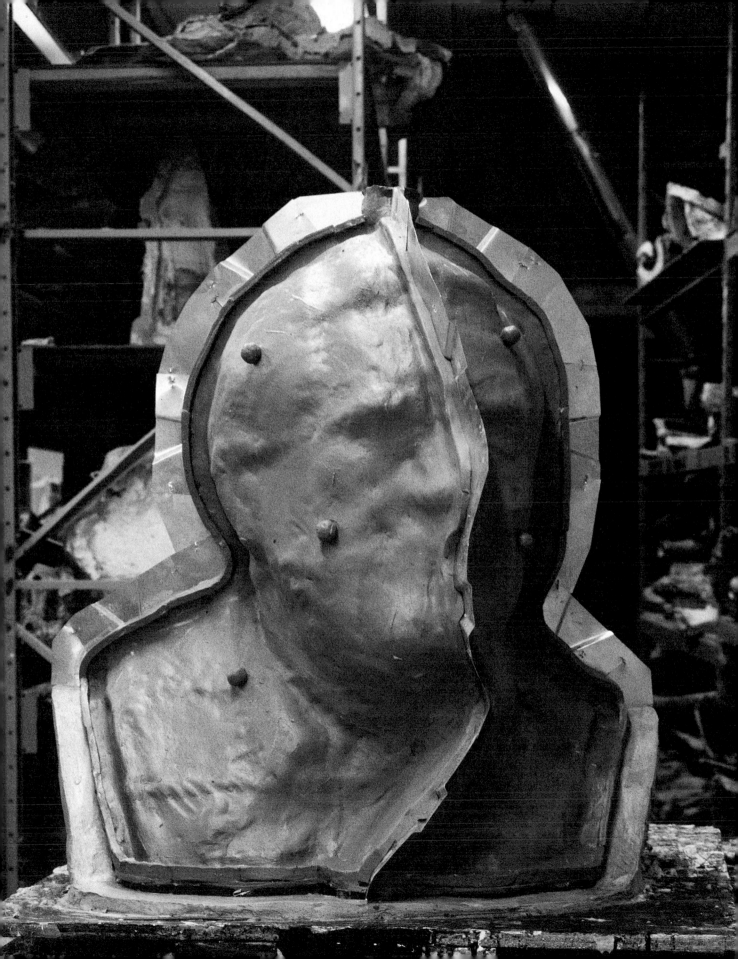

blanket protects the fine details on the face. "We don't want to smash in the eyebrows," says Kurt. "He's got a lot of little stuff sticking out that we have to watch out for." The clay-blanket mold can also be used more than once. A cast of Roosevelt's head will be made from this mold to be shown at the Smithsonian Institution in Washington, D.C., as well.

With clay masking the face, FDR looks like he's wearing a veil. Kurt then uses his bare hands to slather, pat, and dribble liquid plaster all over. "I use my hands instead of a pouring tool to keep air bubbles from being trapped in the plaster," says Kurt, "but the real reason is because that's how the Italians did it hundreds of years ago." When this dries the blanket is removed. Bits of clay are cleaned off the plaster mold which is then shellacked and greased to keep the tuffy from sticking to it. Kurt notes an interesting mathematical fact about this process: "However much the empty mold weighs, that's how many more pounds of tuffy it will take to fill the mold."

It takes the foundry workers three weeks to finish the mother molds for all sections of FDR. It's a muscle-straining, smelly, sticky operation. But great care is taken to get it right, because each detail must be exactly imprinted in the tuffy. It is the mother molds from which the finished sculpture will ultimately come.

When completely dried, the sections of tuffy and plaster are removed from the enlargement and put back together to form an empty mold, or negative. Inside the cavity, foundry workers paint coatings of hot liquid red wax carefully onto each fine surface of the mold, again making sure to cover each detail. Then they fill the cavity using pitchers of molten red wax. The smell of burnt wax fills the room. The wax is allowed to cool slowly to prevent holes from forming inside the figure.

After a few hours, the wax is thoroughly cool. The plaster and black tuffy are pulled off to reveal a startling image: Roosevelt emerges from the mother mold just as he will look in his final form, but in blood-red wax. Neil's first thought upon seeing it is, "This is big! It looks bigger than it did in clay, somehow. I am impressed." Neil is excited to see FDR at this stage. "Up to now, I've just seen him in clay. So colorless and dull. The wax is livelier. It gives me a different perspective. I haven't seen it for awhile because I've been working on Eleanor."

This red-wax positive is taken to the rework room. Here, Tina Jeter is at work again, smoothing the seam lines where the front and back of the head have been joined. This calls for skilled hands and expert judgment. She must make the textures that Neil carved

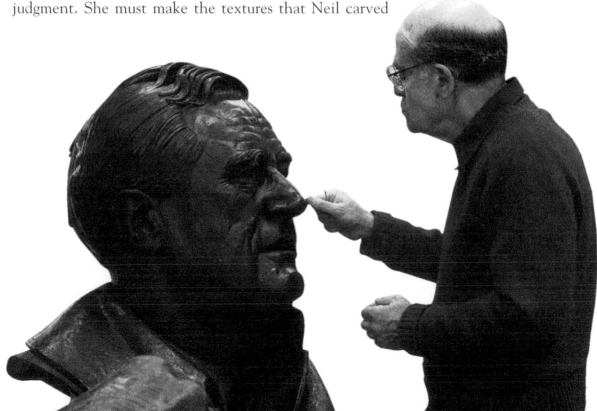

into the clay match exactly on both sides of the line. She also cleans off little globs of black tuffy sticking to the wax, especially in FDR's mouth. Her background as a dental technician comes in handy here, she jokes, though in all seriousness, she says that "moldmaking is the same exact process as working on teeth."

Neil eyes the red-wax head carefully. He's very happy with it. There's not much he must do to correct it, but he will put a few finishing touches to his sculpture directly into the wax. A few freestanding hairs broke off and have to be remodeled. A glob on the lower left of the neck is misshapen. "The tiny changes at the end probably wouldn't make a difference to most people," says Neil. "The sculptor, if he were permitted, will always find something to change. At some point I have to stop, so the work remains in a sense unfinished. If I don't get to make all the changes I'd like to make then maybe that's good."

The red-wax positives are ready for the next molding stage. Each part of the figure must be made ready for filling with molten bronze. To do this, red-wax rods called gates are carefully fixed onto FDR's surface: these will

become feeder tubes for the metal. With all the wax rods in place, FDR looks like a mad scientist has been doing experiments on him.

Next to the rework room is the shell room, a relatively cool and clean room in the foundry where the final molds are made. This process, called dipping, is done by repeatedly dipping the red-wax positive into a vat of ceramic liquid, called the investment material, and letting it harden, much like hand-dipping a candle. After each dipping, the piece receives a coating of zircon sand. After nine days of dipping and cooling, a thick seven-layer shell covers the wax sculpture. At this point FDR looks bizarre—chalky white and hanging from a cooling rack with tubes winding around him and fans blowing on him to harden the mold. Hundreds of sculptures are being processed in the shell room, all of which, including FDR, are photographed and numbered before being sent to an autoclave for baking.

At the heart of the foundry is the huge, hot room where powerful furnaces burn and sparks fly. Here, the autoclave bakes the ceramic shell into a rock-hard investment mold. The oven temperature climbs to 1,200 degrees

Fahrenheit (650 degrees Celsius), so hot that it vaporizes some of the wax. About 100 pounds (45 kilograms) of air pressure inside the oven forces the rest of the wax to stream out of the shell. This is collected for reblending and reuse. Thus the wax is "lost," leaving an empty ceramic mold with built-in tubing.

Once the investment mold cools and it is anchored in the casting pit, the pouring of the bronze can take place. The foundry has three furnaces in which to melt the enormous quantities of metal it needs. The largest can hold up to 3,000 pounds (1,360 kilograms) of the melted metal. Workers in protective silver suits feed stacks of bronze ingots into the roaring furnaces. These ovens reach a blistering 2,800 degrees Fahrenheit (1,540 degrees Celsius). The bronze turns liquid, white-hot. Care is taken to make sure the metal is runny enough to fill the mold precisely. To avoid ruinous air pockets from forming, sometimes the bronze is not actually poured into the mold, but forced through the tubes with air pressure. Pouring is not without risk. It calls for teamwork and split-second timing. The room is sizzling, the equipment is back-breaking, and the end result uncertain.

While foundry workers are busy molding and casting FDR, Neil is in a nearby room fixing problems on Eleanor. Her ankle bones bulge out, too high on the leg. Her shoes are too big. Neil pays a quick visit to the Roosevelt home in nearby Hyde Park to measure the first lady's real shoes. He is determined that his sculptures will be as accurate to the real-life Roosevelts as he can make them. "These changes were not expected," Neil admits. "I'm a little upset with myself. But after looking and looking and looking, it just wasn't right. It has to be right! You can wing it with a small model, but when it's big, there's no faking it."

The enlargement process has left parts of Eleanor's face, arms and hands off-kilter as well. "Too fleshy," says Neil. He gets busy measuring every point on the Eleanor scale model with calipers, and comparing this measurement to the same place on the enlargement. Even a quarter-inch matters. When he finds an area where not enough clay has been left, he adds clay; where too much clay has been left, he scrapes and shapes it. "It's very tiresome," says the weary sculptor, "but if I don't check everything and correct these little errors, the whole thing will be thrown off balance."

While the foundry work goes on, a huge team of workers is busy in Washington, D.C., building the memorial. The construction site takes up 7.5 scenic acres (3 hectares) on the banks of the Potomac Tidal Basin. The

attractive Jefferson Memorial is just across the water to the right. To the left towers the Washington Monument. Army helicopters roar low overhead, taking the president's staff back and forth to the White House nearby. Washington's famous old cherry trees line the Tidal Basin walkway in front of the FDR Memorial. The place is beautiful and exciting all at once.

The memorial is being built back-to-front. By late October, the Depression section is still far from finished. The area where Neil's sculptures will be, the World War II section, is nearly done. Blocks of granite have been made into thick walls. Words and quotes from speeches that Roosevelt made while president are being carved into the stone with an alphabet designed for the memorial by John Benson. So much stone is used, and so many piles of stone still wait to be placed, that it almost seems like the Great Pyramids are being built. The niches that will hold Neil's sculptures are ready and waiting. This is an exciting moment for Neil, who pays a visit to the memorial site. Playfully, the sculptor poses himself in Eleanor's spot, as the first lady, while his wife snaps a picture of him. But the sculptor's fun is brief. He must hurry back to work at the foundry.

The moment of truth: the bronze has cooled. It is time to reveal the finished Roosevelt. The great block is hoisted from the pit and taken to the knock-out area. Wearing hard hats and masks,

foundry workers use brute force to knock away the shell. "It's kind of like watching the chicken come out of the egg," says Neil. The "egg" is not easily cracked. The din of sledgehammers, picks, chisels, and finally sandblasters rings out as the layers come off to reveal the raw bronze sculpture of Franklin Delano Roosevelt.

The artist is relieved and joyful to see his sculpture at last. Neil closely inspects it for imperfections in the surface. Small holes are welded over. Larger holes are fixed by cutting out the area and recasting it. Then comes what Neil calls "the great conundrum." He watches over the fitting together of the pieces. This is like doing a weighty three-dimensional jigsaw puzzle. Sometimes pieces must be bent to make them fit.

Tallix Foundry workers weld the pieces together. The weld marks are smoothed out with a chasing tool to imitate the surrounding surface. No polishing or buffing is done. Neil wants the rough workings of the tools to show in his sculpture. Heat and acids are applied to give the bronze a pale, antique-green color called a patina. Wax is applied to keep off rain and chemicals in the environment.

It is April 17, 1997, deadline day for Neil, and reality finally hits him. He's done. Really done! Grin after grin spreads across his face. Neil and his wife throw a party in the enlarging rooms while workers are wrapping the sculptures for shipping. Neil makes a speech: "Thank you for all your dedicated hard work and skill," he tells the foundry artisans. "It's been a unique experience. Thank you." Glasses of champagne are raised in triumph.

The sculptures are thickly wrapped and carefully hoisted onto a flatbed tractor-trailer. Roosevelt's final weight is 3,300 pounds (1,500 kg), heavy enough to be a wrecking ball if it should topple. A crew drives five hours through the night from Beacon, N.Y., to Washington, D.C., to be at the memorial site in the morning. Along the way, says Richard Fazio, the crew foreman, "We go up to a tollbooth and motorists say, 'What's back there?' I say, 'Follow us!'"

"If only I had a little more time," muses the sculptor, "there are still improvements I could make." Nevertheless, the job is done at last. "I consider this to be the pinnacle of my career, such as it is. It is the work that I have the biggest personal investment in. It will be visited by millions of

people, so I'm very aware of having to do the best work I can. It's both a challenge, creatively, and a burden. I've had to gather material, study it, analyze the personalities, and decide how to present it. It isn't simply a waxwork figure. It has to have validity as a work of art, not rest solely on the fame of those it depicts. I hope the public thinks I caught the essential man."

Neil meets the crew at the site. Because heavy cranes would tear up the new landscaping, a wheeled platform is used to roll Roosevelt and the others to their niches. This is no easy job, as they have a few corners to turn.

A hush among the collected onlookers erupts into a gasp of recognition as the wrappings come off. A delighted Lawrence Halprin, the architect, throws his arms around Neil. He and the sculptor then spend two entire days rolling the statues from side to side, adjusting and readjusting the position of each sculpture. When they are at last satisfied, an exhausted Neil breathes a sigh of tremendous relief. As people crowd around FDR on opening day, May 2, 1997, the artist muses, "How can I ever top this?"

FRANKLIN DELANO ROOSEVELT
JANUARY 30, 1882-APRIL 12, 1945

F ranklin Delano Roosevelt, or FDR, was the only child of a wealthy New York family. He served as a New York state senator from 1911-1913, and then was appointed assistant secretary of the United States Navy. He married his distant cousin, Anna Eleanor Roosevelt, in 1905. They had five children. Then in 1921, FDR was struck with poliomyelitis. The disease paralyzed him from the waist down. For the rest of his life, he never regained the use of his legs.

Roosevelt's condition did not deter him from a career in public service. In 1928 he was elected governor. In 1933 FDR was elected the thirty-second president of the United States. It was then he began his famous "fireside chats" over the radio, the first American president ever to use this mass medium to talk directly to the people. With his beloved dog Fala at his feet, he discussed America's economic problems and outlined his plans for the future. Americans put great faith in these promises. He had told people in his first inaugural address that "the only thing we have to fear is fear itself."

FDR's popularity and political shrewdness made him the only U.S. president ever to be elected four times, serving from 1933 to 1945. Roosevelt handled the two biggest crises in American history. First was the aftermath of the stock-market crash of 1929 and, following that, the Great Depression. Almost fifteen million Americans lost their jobs. Millions of people lost all their money, their homes, their businesses, and their hopes for the future.

To turn the country around, Roosevelt, for the first time in American history, made the federal government a major agent of social change. He promised the country a "New Deal." The New Deal was a group of government programs that gave jobs to millions of unemployed Americans. The most famous of these was the Works Projects Administration (WPA). FDR passed the National Labor Relations Act, which allowed workers in labor unions to bargain on equal terms with bosses. He established the minimum wage. He also passed the Social Security program. This guaranteed a retirement pension for all Americans. This assistance helped to restore faith in the government at a time when the nation seemed on the brink of economic collapse.

Eleanor, meanwhile, served as her husband's eyes and ears around the nation. She traveled ceaselessly on housing, education, and labor inspections. Her reports to FDR helped him push through laws that helped the poor, homeless, jobless, and uneducated. Eleanor also worked bravely to stop discrimination against African Americans. She was far ahead of her time in demanding equal rights for blacks in housing, education, and voting. Her groundbreaking work made her unpopular among wealthier taxpayers, but to the millions she tried to help she was regarded as almost a saint. After FDR's death she was appointed America's first ambassador to the United Nations by President Harry Truman.

Many Americans thought Roosevelt's policies were too radical. The New Deal, they argued, made too many people rely on the government for help. This raised taxes for everyone. Some even accused the Roosevelts and members of their administration of sympathizing with communists. Nevertheless, Roosevelt's model of government is essentially still in use. From the New Deal era come welfare, public housing, education loans, large public works, and all kinds of government protections for the jobs, health, and safety of workers.

Just as the Depression showed signs of lifting, World War II struck Europe. Many Americans tried to look the other way. FDR went against majority opinion. He tried to help Great Britain and the Soviet Union fight the Nazi invasion with the Lend-Lease Act, which let these countries borrow weapons and army bases. He was accused of trying to drag America into the war. Then, on December 7, 1941, "a date which will live in infamy," said Roosevelt, everything changed. Japan bombed the U.S. military base at Pearl Harbor, Hawaii. More than two thousand were killed, the Pacific navy was shattered, and America was thrust into World War II.

Under Roosevelt's firm leadership, America rallied all of its power to win the war. His charisma and confidence helped sustain the American people in this turbulent period. Together with allies Winston Churchill of Great Britain and Joseph Stalin of the Soviet Union, he mapped out war strategy. He also gave the go-ahead for the development of the most powerful and destructive weapon in history, the atom bomb. After twelve years as president (four of them at war), and a mere three weeks before the Allied victory in Europe, Roosevelt died of a brain hemorrhage in Warm Springs, Georgia, on April 12, 1945.

GLOSSARY

armature: the flexible wire and wood framework that supports the clay, wax, or plaster as it is being sculpted.

autoclave: an oven that uses high pressure and steam.

black tuffy: a rubberlike compound put on the finished model to make a mold.

bronze: a metal alloy made by combining copper and up to 11 percent tin.

bust: a sculpture of a person's head and shoulders.

caliper: a tool with adjustable arms that measures the thicknesses and distances between points on a surface.

casting: the process of filling a negative (empty) mold with wax, metal, or plaster to make a positive form.

foundry: a factory where metal is melted, poured, and formed.

gating: covering the red-wax positive with liquid ceramic by dipping and cooling repeatedly.

ingot: a brick-sized bar of metal.

investment: the final mold, made by covering the wax positive with a liquid ceramic called the "investment material."

lost-wax technique: once the investment mold hardens, it is baked, and the red wax runs out, leaving a durable ceramic mold into which the bronze can be poured to get a final metal cast.

maquette: a small, three-dimensional model for a sculptural or architectural project.

model: an image in clay, wax, or plaster on which a finished sculpture of the same image is based.

monument: a statue, building, pillar, or other thing erected in memory of a person or event.

mother mold: the first mold, created by the application of black tuffy to the final model, into which wax is poured to make the red-wax positive.

patina: surface color or finish.

plaster: the powder form of the mineral gypsum, which, when mixed with water, can be formed into shapes and dried solid.

plastiline: sculptor's synthetic clay that never dries out, used in making models.

pointing: the process of creating an exact enlargement of the scale model in clay using a pointing tool that precisely marks the corresponding points from the smaller model to the larger model.

polio: an infectious disease that attacks the motor nerves in the spine and brain, resulting in paralysis of the limbs and skeletal deformity; polio is now controlled with a vaccine.

positive: the product that comes out of the mold (the mold is the negative, much like a photo negative, which, when printed, results in a positive picture).

rebar: steel reinforcement bars added to the mother mold to keep it from shifting.

scale: the proportion or size of an object in relation to other objects.

sculpture: a work of art created by carving, molding, welding, or constructing materials to make a three-dimensional form.

studio: an artist's workroom, usually a very large, well-lighted space.

three-dimensional: any object having, or seeming to have, height, width, and depth, that is, something that does not appear flat.

zircon: a semi-precious mineral.

INDEX

ABOUT THE ARTIST

The works of Neil Estern capture the subtle elements that animate a specific personality with a presence as unique as a fingerprint. Some of his commissioned works include a recently erected figure of Fiorello LaGuardia, a bust of John F. Kennedy, and portraits of J. Edgar Hoover, Jimmy Carter, Calvin Vaux, Frederick Law Olmstead, and Danny Kaye. Estern's works are in numerous private collections and can be seen in the Brooklyn Museum.

ABOUT THE AUTHOR

Kelli Peduzzi has been a freelance editor for fourteen years. Currently she is an editor for Highlights Plus. *Shaping a President* is the fourth book she has written for children. She lives in New York.

ABOUT THE PHOTOGRAPHER

Diane Smook is a professional photographer with many exhibition and gallery credits. She has been a television and video producer. This is her first book. She lives in New York City.